THE CUNARD COLOURING BOOK

First published 2018

The History Press
The Mill, Brimscombe Port
Stroud, Gloucestershire, GL5 2QG
www.thehistorypress.co.uk

British Library Cataloguing in Publication Data.
A catalogue record for this book is available from the British Library.

ISBN 978 0 7509 9002 8

Typesetting and origination by The History Press
Printed in Turkey by Imak

THE CUNARD COLOURING BOOK

WITH CHRIS FRAME & RACHELLE CROSS

The History Press

Cunard Line was founded in 1839 by Halifax-born entrepreneur Samuel Cunard. The line originally traded under the name of British and North American Royal Mail Steam Packet Co., but quickly became known as 'Cunard's Line'. In July 1840, Cunard commenced the world's first regular transatlantic steam crossings. Their first purpose-built ship, *Britannia*, was a paddle steamer and took fourteen days to cross the North Atlantic from Liverpool to Boston. The line expanded quickly as the new service proved a success.

The Cunard livery was established early on, with a distinctive orange-red selected for the funnels, a colour that would be called 'Cunard red'. The funnel sections were divided by black bands and the top section was painted black to disguise soot and smoke stains. From those early days the hulls of the ships were painted a dark, almost black, hue, which helped to retain heat on the frigid North Atlantic.

Samuel Cunard insisted that his captains operate their vessels with the primary purpose of safely delivering passengers, cargo and their ship each and every crossing. This culture of safety became embedded in the company and endures to this day. Cunard has weathered many changes over the years, including two world wars, stiff competition from the introduction of air travel and several changes in ownership. Today the Cunard name lives on, with their three ships: *Queen Mary 2, Queen Victoria* and *Queen Elizabeth*.

Mauretania (stamp)

In 1907 Cunard launched their 'Ocean Greyhounds', *Mauretania* and *Lusitania*. Though built to the same general schematic, *Mauretania* was distinguishable by her oversized scoop air vents positioned on her top deck. She was a very fast ship, fitted with Parsons turbines and four propellers, and captured the Blue Riband for fastest westbound transatlantic crossing in 1909. She held it until 1929. (Original image courtesy Cunard)

Lusitania and *Mauretania* (poster)

When *Lusitania* and *Mauretania* entered service in 1907 they were the largest ships in the world. They primarily traded on the transatlantic using the port of Liverpool. In 1919, when Cunard changed their home port to Southampton, *Mauretania* inaugurated the service. *Lusitania* was lost during First World War whilst in civilian service off the coast of Cobh, Ireland. (Original image courtesy Cunard)

Mauretania (postcard)

The second *Mauretania* was launched in 1938 at the Cammell Laird yard in Birkenhead, England, and was the first ship built for the newly merged Cunard-White Star Line. *Mauretania* was requisitioned for trooping duties during the Second World War. In addition she was used for the war bride repatriation service following the cessation of hostilities. She retired from service in 1965 and was broken up. (Original image courtesy Cunard)

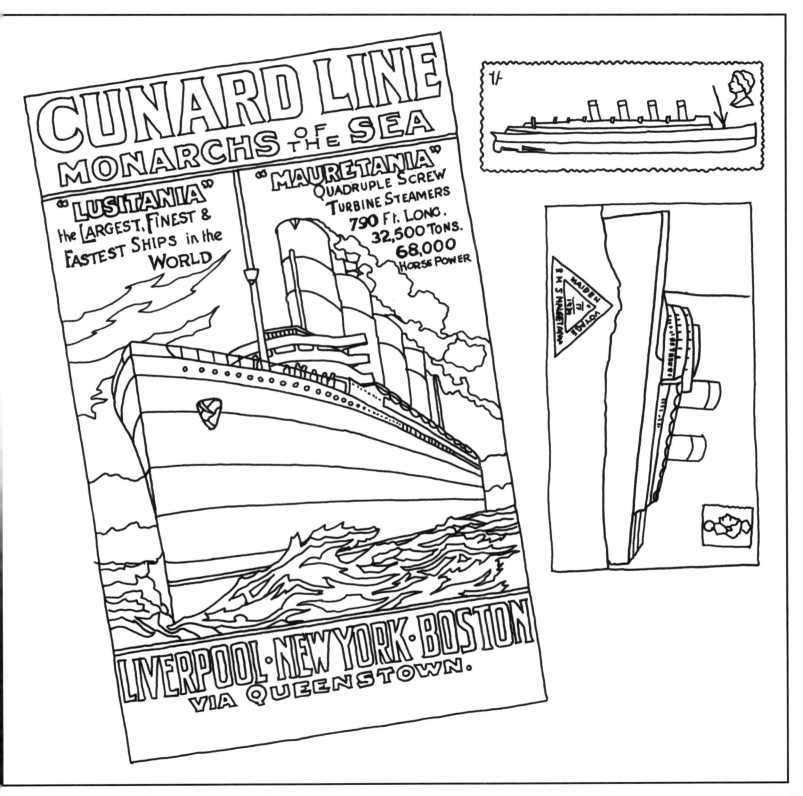

Mauretania

When *Mauretania* captured the Blue Riband in 1909, she did so with an average speed of 26.06 knots. To achieve this speed she utilised 25 boilers with 192 furnaces that drove her Parsons steam turbines; this large number of furnaces required four funnels to ventilate her boiler rooms. The funnels were painted in the traditional Cunard red, with the uppermost section painted black, disguising the soot stains. (Original image courtesy Cunard)

Carpathia

Carpathia was built at C.S. Swan & Hunter, Newcastle upon Tyne. She was an intermediate liner, never destined to break records for size or speed. However, *Carpathia* became one of the most famous Cunard ships of her day when she rescued the survivors of the *Titanic* on 15 April 1912. Following this she attracted a loyal following. *Carpathia* sunk during the First World War after being torpedoed by *U-55*. (Original image courtesy Cunard)

Aquitania

Aquitania was launched on 30 May 1914 at the John Brown Shipyard in Clydebank, Scotland. She was the largest and longest serving of the Cunard four stackers, and served in both world wars. She was much loved by the public, who gave her the nickname 'Ship Beautiful'. The ship was painted in the traditional Cunard colours, with the lower part of her funnels painted Cunard red and the top section painted black. (Original image courtesy Cunard)

Queen Mary

Queen Mary was laid down in December 1930, but construction was halted twelve months later due to the effects of the Great Depression. Works finally resumed in 1934 and she was launched that same year. *Queen Mary* won the speed record from *Normandie* in 1936 and again in 1938, this time holding it until 1952. She was retired in 1967 and is now a floating hotel in Longbeach, California. (Original image courtesy Cunard)

Queen Elizabeth

Beginning her career as a troop transport during the Second World War, *Queen Elizabeth* commenced her passenger service career in 1946. Designated RMS (Royal Mail Ship) she was the largest liner in the world when she entered service. Unlike modern-day ships she did not have bow and stern thrusters, instead requiring multiple tugs to assist in manoeuvring her during port arrivals and departures. (Original image courtesy Cunard)

QE2's Stern

As *QE2* was designed in the 1960s she had a classic ocean liner appearance. The aft end of her superstructure was terraced, providing many vantage points for passengers to view the lower decks as well as the sea. Shelter was provided by windows on One, Quarter and Upper Decks, while Boat Deck housed the Sports Centre. *QE2* was the first of Cunard's Queens to be registered in Southampton, which remained her homeport throughout her Cunard career.

QE2 at the Overseas Passenger Terminal, Sydney

Due to her height, *QE2* was unable to fit under the Sydney Harbour Bridge; thus when she visited Sydney she docked at the Overseas Passenger Terminal in Circular Quay. Tugs would manoeuvre her in, with her bow facing out, allowing for an easier departure. Her bridge wings were open, giving her bridge officers great sightlines both forward and aft. Whilst in port she would take on marine diesel from a bunkering vessel, which would tie up alongside.

QE2's Boat Deck

Unlike modern cruise ships, QE2's Boat Deck was open, with the lifeboats set above on davits. The forward-most lifeboat on each side of the ship was painted red and used for fast response situations. The ship's boat deck was clad in real teak wood, with dark green gutters to handle run-off water, while her superstructure was white and supported the black funnel, which was surrounded by red cowling.

QE2's Forward Profile

QE2 was designed to undertake regular transatlantic crossings. As a result she was built with a long bow, with her bridge set on the highest level of her superstructure. The hull was painted black (federal grey), which helped to disguise wear and tear. Her boot top was painted red, with a white dividing line between the two. The top of the bow and her superstructure were painted white, which gave her a very traditional ocean liner appearance.

QE2's Funnel

In 1986–87 *QE2* was given a new diesel electric power plant. To accommodate these works her funnel was removed and the old machinery was lifted out of the engine room. Once her new engines were in place, a new funnel was built, utilising some of the pieces from the original. The new structure was wider than the original and painted black, with a red cowling that sported two black stripes.

Queen Elizabeth 2

QE2's Lifeboats

QE2's lifeboats were designed in the 1960s and, as a result, not all were enclosed. When she retired QE2 had ten open lifeboats, four semi-covered lifeboats and six tenders. The two rapid response boats were painted red, while the remainder of the boats were painted white with black trim and orange interiors. For the first half of her career QE2's lifeboat davits were painted grey, but this was later changed to white.

QE2's 'White Horses of the Atlantic'

Located on Upper Deck, *QE2*'s Mauretania Restaurant offered two seatings at dinner time and open seating at both breakfast and lunch. Named for the 1907 *Mauretania*, the restaurant centrepiece was an aluminium resin statue depicting the 'White Horses of the Atlantic' that had been created by Althea Wynne. The statue was lit from below with blue light to simulate water.

QE2's Midships Lobby

QE2's embarkation lobby was situated on Two Deck. The room featured a sunken lounge with built-in seating upholstered in blue. This surrounded a white trumpet column, which supported a mirrored ceiling. The carpet was burgundy and red and the curtains, which concealed the shell doors, were also a dark red. The walls were panelled in wood veneer and were home to four large murals by Peter Sutton, depicting the history of the Cunard Line.

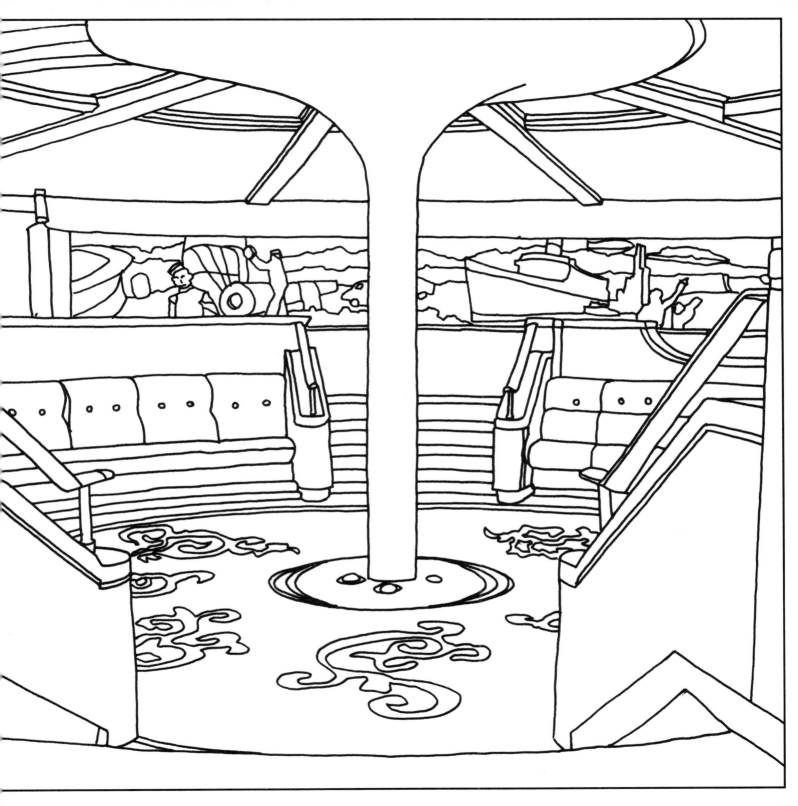

QE2 alongside in Piraeus

QE2 was designed as a dual-purpose liner, meaning she was able to undertake line voyages as well as regular cruises. Her design included a long, strong steel-hulled bow, which was painted black, while her white superstructure was made from aluminium. Her dual-purpose design allowed the ship to operate part of the year on the North Atlantic while also visiting numerous warm-weather ports. The second tallest point on the ship was her mast, which was 51.54m above the waterline.

QE2 in Sydney, 2008

The Cunard ships are regular visitors to the port of Sydney, Australia. In 2008 *QE2* made her final call in Sydney, thirty years to the day of her first arrival in 1978. She berthed at the Overseas Passenger Terminal in Circular Quay, giving her passengers a spectacular view of the Harbour Bridge from her forward observation platforms. The bow of the ship was pale grey, with black anchor supports and white capstans and anchor chains.

Caronia

The third Cunard ship to bear the name *Caronia*, this ship began her service career as *Vistafjord* for Norwegian America Line. Launched in 1973, she was the last cruise ship to be built in Britain. *Vistafjord* joined the Cunard fleet ten years later, along with her sister ship *Sagafjord*. In 1999 Cunard gave her a significant refurbishment and renamed her *Caronia*. During this refurbishment, her pebble-grey hull was repainted in the darker Cunard colour. (Original image courtesy Cunard)

Caronia

At 24,292 gross registered tons and 191.09m long, *Caronia* was significantly smaller than all of the ships in Cunard's fleet today. *Caronia* left the Cunard fleet in 2004, following Cunard placing an order for a new Vista-class cruise ship, and she was sold to Saga Cruises, where she re-joined her former fleet mate *Sagafjord*. The two ships were renamed *Saga Ruby* and *Saga Rose*. (Original image courtesy Cunard)

Saga Ruby (formerly *Caronia* and *Vistafjord*)

Following her withdrawal from Cunard service, *Caronia* commenced cruising for Saga Cruises. Renamed *Saga Ruby*, she was paired with *Saga Rose*, the former Cunard *Sagafjord*. Both ships were painted in the Saga Cruises livery of dark blue hull, white superstructure and yellow funnel with a dark blue top separated by a white stripe. Whilst *Saga Rose* was retired in 2009, *Saga Ruby* continued to sail until 2014.

The former *Royal Viking Sun*

In 1994 Cunard acquired *Royal Viking Sun*, at that time one of the highest-rated ships in the world. After the acquisition of Cunard by Carnival, *Royal Viking Sun* was moved to the Seabourn fleet, also owned by Carnival. She was later transferred to Holland America Line, where she was repainted in their dark blue and white livery and renamed *Prinsendam*. In 2010 *QM2* met *Prinsendam* in Barcelona whilst they were both undertaking Mediterranean cruises.

QM2's Profile

QM2 was the first transatlantic ocean liner built since *QE2* and was designed to resemble her older fleet mate. However, at 345m long and with thirteen passenger decks, *QM2* is a much larger ship than *QE2*. Travellers' expectations had evolved since *QE2*'s build and the high demand for balcony cabins led to the addition of traditional balconies as well as 'hull hole' balconies that were embedded in the ship's hull.

QM2's Stern

QM2's stern shape has been an object of much discussion since her entry into service in 2004. The shape is a hybrid between a cruiser stern (rounded) and a transom stern (square), known as a 'Costanzi' stern, named for the designer who pioneered this shape. It allows for the best positioning of her propeller pods, whilst also giving her a more traditional-looking aft appearance.

QM2's Spa

The spa aboard *QM2* is the perfect place to relax. The water in the large hydrotherapy pool reflects the light blue backlit ceiling above. The pool is surrounded by a dark wooden bench that extends to the raised whirlpool in the corner. The room is tiled in cream with the colour echoed in the coffered ceiling. This room is a calm oasis with potted bamboo, shell sculptures and the soothing sound of falling water.

QM2's Planetarium

QM2's planetarium is named Illuminations and is accessed from Deck 3. It is the only planetarium at sea, with a domed screen that descends from the ceiling when in use. The room is also used as a movie theatre, with 3D projectors, and is the primary lecture venue. The seating in this room is colour-coded, with the chairs below the planetarium screen dark red, whilst the rest of the chairs are gold.

QM2's Balmoral Suite

One of the four grand suites aboard QM2, the Balmoral Suite is decorated in a largely neutral colour palette. The separate lounge area features light wood-panelled walls, offset by dark wood furniture and door trims. A light-coloured sofa faces the TV, whilst red accents are picked out on the desk chair, cushions and flowers. The suite has its own deck area, viewed and accessed by the glass windows and door on the aft wall.

QM2's Britannia Restaurant

The grandest room aboard the *QM2* is the Britannia Restaurant. Three storeys tall, it is crowned by a stunning gold-toned light-well. The light-coloured columns have a marble effect, while the upper deck surround, balustrades and wine cabinets are finished in glossy mid-toned wood veneers. The carpets are richly coloured in blue, turquoise and gold tones. On the lower level the chairs are upholstered in a russet colour, whilst those on the upper levels are tan.

QM2 Arrives in Fremantle

QM2 is 345m long; as a result, in some of the ports she visits there are technical difficulties to overcome when docking. In the port of Fremantle, Western Australia, *QM2* docks bow out. Because of her length and the clearance required to execute the 180-degree turn, special consideration needs to be made to which other ships are in the port at the time.

QM2's Maiden Departure from Fremantle

QM2 undertook her first world cruise in 2007. It was a great success and she has repeated it many times since. Her maiden call at the port of Fremantle was made in March 2010. As she was the largest ship to visit the port to that date she caused a sensation, with many locals taking advantage of the sunny evening to come out and watch the ship depart.

QM2's Grand Lobby

QM2's Grand Lobby is five storeys tall and houses the Purser's Office and Shore Tours Office. The room is striking, with a bold sunburst design on its carpet that features geometric rays of cream, red, gold and grey. This is juxtaposed with cream-coloured plasterwork and chairs, and a black baby grand piano. A large fresh flower display on a brown stone table forms the centrepiece of the room.

QM2's Carinthia Lounge

QM2's Carinthia Lounge was created during the 2016 refit in the space previously occupied by the Winter Garden. Now a popular coffee lounge and port bar, the Carinthia Lounge is a light and bright space, finished in gold tones with the occasional splash of blue from accent chairs. The decorative gold screen features a pattern of the letters 'C' and 'L' repeated in both directions, while the walls are painted beige.

QE2 and *Queen Victoria*

On 24 February 2008 *QE2* and *Queen Victoria* met in Sydney Harbour. It was *Queen Victoria*'s first visit to the port, and *QE2*'s last. Hundreds of boats and thousands of people turned out to watch the two ships pass by each other near Fort Dennison. *QE2*'s classic 1960s ocean liner design was a stark contrast to *Queen Victoria*'s modern cruise ship appearance.

Queen Victoria alongside in Sydney

Berthed bow-in at Circular Quay's Overseas Passenger Terminal, _Queen Victoria_ is close to popular icons such as the Sydney Harbour Bridge and Opera House. During some world cruises the ship will remain alongside overnight, allowing passengers the opportunity to enjoy the Sydney nightlife and explore the city in more depth. This location puts the ship close to the ferry terminal for easy access to Manly Beach and Darling Harbour.

Queen Victoria's Royal Court Theatre

Red is the colour of *Queen Victoria*'s Royal Court Theatre, with the hue carried through the stage curtains, seating and carpeting of this three-storey venue. When introduced in 2007 the ship was the first to offer theatre boxes, which are fronted in gold tint. This venue is utilised throughout the day and night, as the primary show lounge, movie theatre and lecture venue.

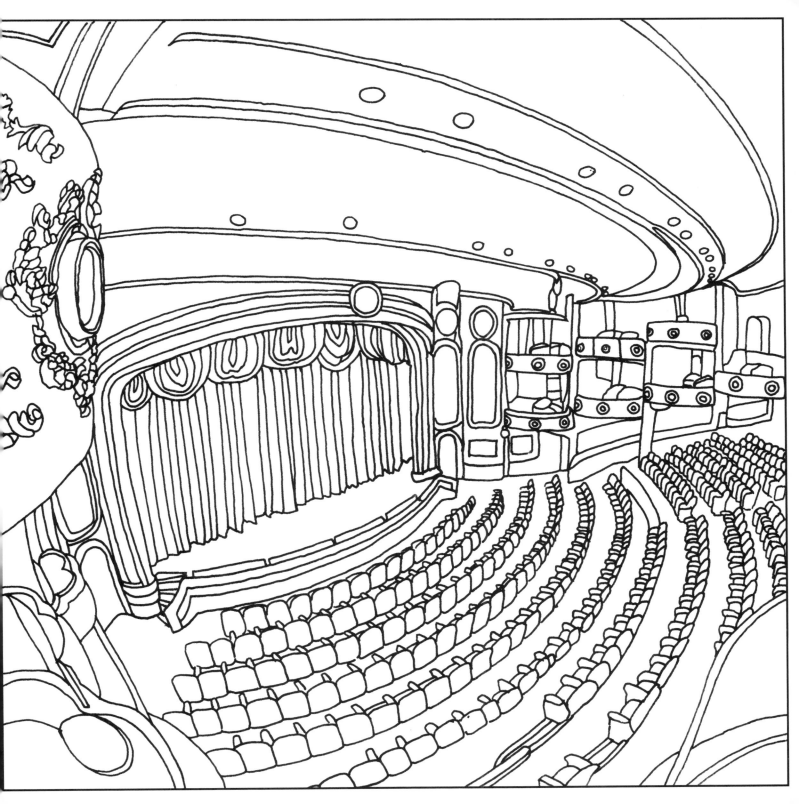

Queen Victoria's **Winter Garden**

Queen Victoria's Winter Garden is bathed in natural light from its glass ceiling. The room is carpeted in a vibrant blue, with orange detail, and has a view out to the Pavillion Pool. The garden theme is brought to life by wicker furniture with blue cushions and greenery in the form of palms and a central tree. Drinks are available throughout the day and into the evening and so it is a popular venue for watching sporting events on the large screens.

Queen Victoria's Britannia Cabin

Queen Victoria's Britannia cabins were originally fitted out in a neutral colour scheme, with accent pillows of burgundy or dark blue depending on which side of the ship the room was located. The doors, closets, writing desk and chair, coffee table and bedside tables were all finished in a light wood veneer while the bedhead had a black border surrounding the same light-coloured wood. In 2017 the cabins were updated and given a more modern appearance.

Grills Lounge aboard *Queen Victoria*

Those dining in the Queens Grill and Princess Grill restaurants are welcomed to the Grills Lounge. The bar is finished in dark wood tones with navy bar stools, and comfortable tan and cream chairs sit beneath a domed light well. The focal point of the room, this light well is patterned in a green-on-cream floral and leaf motif, with an orange flower design in the centre of the feature. Below and above the light panels are dark wooden mouldings.

***Queen Victoria*'s Grand Lobby**

The Grand Lobby aboard *Queen Victoria* spans three decks and is dominated by a bas-relief by John McKenna that depicts the ship at sea, set against a wooden marquetry panel. Stairs carpeted in brown tones connect the various decks, with light-coloured stone, plasterwork and tiles offsetting the darker tones in this space. Topiaries sit on each side of the central staircase, while the balustrades and railings are finished in dark metal and mid-toned wood.

Queen Victoria's Pavilion Pool

Refreshed during the ship's 2017 refit, the Pavilion Pool is tiled in light blue with a darker purple surround. The tile surround features a wave pattern in white, blue and teal. Surrounding the pool are charcoal and grey deck chairs, while wicker furniture with brightly coloured cushions spill out from the nearby Winter Garden. During warm weather cruises the Pavilion Pool is a very popular location due to its sheltered aspect.

Queen Elizabeth Marquetry Panel

A main feature of *Queen Elizabeth*'s Grand Lobby is the 5.6m-high marquetry panel depicting the original RMS *Queen Elizabeth* on a backdrop of the North Atlantic Ocean. Created by David Linley, the panel includes nine different types of wood veneer. The panel is surrounded by a cream arch and overlooks the main stairway of the lobby. It is flanked by two topiaries while fresh flowers are on display in the centre of the lobby.

Queen Elizabeth's **Library**

Spanning two decks, with an illuminated wooden spiral staircase, the library aboard *Queen Elizabeth* is popular with travellers. Whilst part of the lower level has a wooden floor, the majority of both levels are carpeted in a light turquoise and cream pattern with a tawny border, colours which are echoed in the stained-glass ceiling. The walls are panelled in mid-toned wood veneer with darker wooden accents.

Queen Elizabeth's Pavilion Pool

Located amidships on Deck 9, the Pavilion Pool and its surround are tiled in pale blue. It is bordered by a polished wooden bench, while wooden stairs at the forward end lead up to raised whirlpools. The heavily tinted windows of the Yacht Club overlook the pool, and above this can be seen the ship's mast, which flies the flags of Cunard, the Red Ensign and whichever country the ship is visiting.

Queen Elizabeth's Queens Room

Queen Elizabeth's ballroom, called 'the Queens Room', is a lavish space aboard the ship. Featuring a large wooden dance floor, with a paler-coloured patterned inlay, the room is given extra glamour by its art deco-style crystal chandeliers. The stage sits behind midnight-blue curtains that hang the full double height of this room, while along the port side are stained-glass light panels in yellow and brown tones.

Queen Elizabeth's Promenade Deck

Classic wooden steamer deck chairs add a traditional touch to *Queen Elizabeth's* promenade deck. They are padded with royal blue cushions that display the Cunard emblem in white. Though located within the hull of the ship, the walls are painted white to help to give a sense of space, despite the overhanging lifeboats. The deck is a faux-wood finish, and is lighter than the real-wood cabinets in the corner that are used to store additional lifejackets.

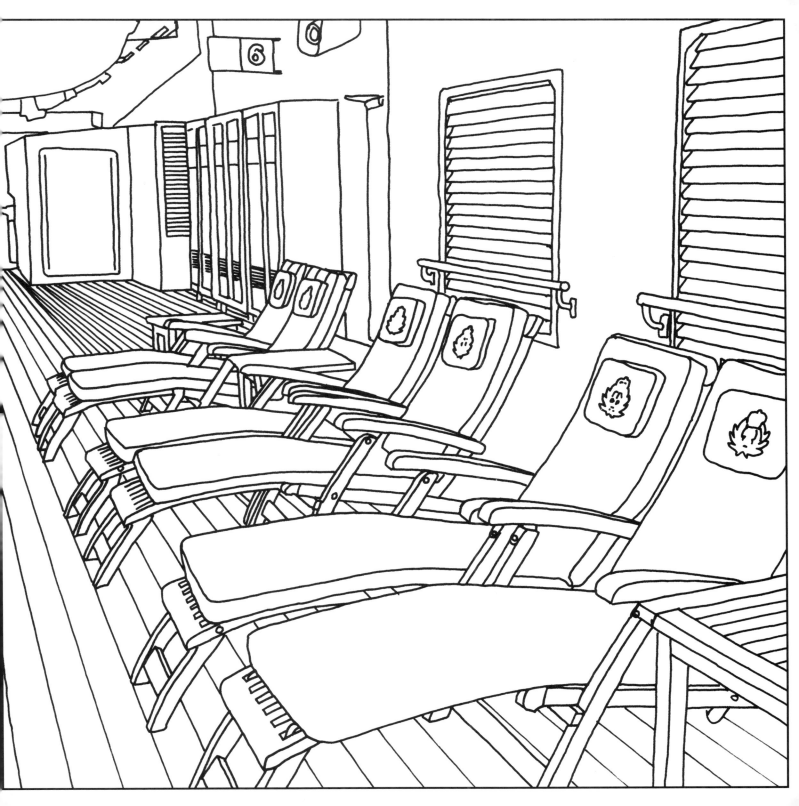

Queen Elizabeth's **Verandah Restaurant**

The Verandah Restaurant is an extra tariff restaurant located on Deck 2. Featuring white chairs and silver and white table settings, the room has a warm and inviting feel. The artwork depicts brightly coloured circus scenes in contrast to the more muted neutral tones of the room. The finishes in this room focus on silver, glass and mirrored surfaces with a brown and cream patterned carpet.

Cunard Steamship Company Emblem

For much of Cunard's existence the company was officially known as The Cunard
Steamship Company, and key elements of the current logo date back to Victorian
times. The logo depicts a rampant crowned lion holding the globe with the North
Atlantic Ocean in view. This Victorian-style logo is displayed aboard the *Queen Victoria*
in the Grand Lobby on Deck 1. Finished in gold, it is displayed on a dark-wood wall.

Thank you to Andrea Lenihan and Emma Jarvis from Cunard for providing historical imagery. All images unless otherwise noted were based on original photographs taken by Chris Frame and Rachelle Cross. Historical Cunard information in this book can be viewed in depth in *175 Years of Cunard* by Chris Frame and Rachelle Cross (The History Press) or online at www.chriscunard.com

Share your creation with the hashtag #cunardcolouringbook